Spelling
Practice Book

Grade 1

Harcourt
SCHOOL PUBLISHERS

www.harcourtschool.com

ISBN 10   0-15-349896-X
ISBN 13   978-0-15-349896-1

11 12 13 14 15 16 1421 16 15 14 13 12 11
4500295671

Contents

SPRING FORWARD—BOOK 1-1

Lesson 1 Short Vowel /a/*a* 1
Lesson 2 Short Vowel /a/*a* 4
Lesson 3 Short Vowel /i/*i* 7
Theme 1 Test 10
Lesson 4 Digraph /k/*ck* 12
Lesson 5 Short Vowel /o/*o* 15
Lesson 6 Variant Vowel /ô/*a* (*all*) 18
Theme 2 Test 21

ZOOM ALONG—BOOK 1-2

Lesson 7 Short Vowel /e/*e* 23
Lesson 8 Digraph /th/*th* 26
Lesson 9 Short Vowel /u/*u* 29
Lesson 10 Diphthong /ng/*ng* 32
Lesson 11 *r*-Controlled Vowel /ôr/*or, ore* 35
Lesson 12 Digraph /sh/*sh* 38
Theme 3 Test 41

REACH FOR THE STARS—BOOK 1-3

Lesson 13 Digraphs /ch/*ch, tch* 43
Lesson 14 *r*-Controlled Vowel /är/*ar* 46
Lesson 15 Digraphs /kw/*qu*, /hw/*wh* 49
Lesson 16 *r*-Controlled Vowels /ûr/*er, ir, ur* 52
Lesson 17 Syllable /əl/*-le* 55
Lesson 18 Long Vowel /ō/*ow, oa* 58
Theme 4 Test 61

Contents

MAKE YOUR MARK—BOOK 1-4

Lesson 19 Long Vowel /ē/e, ee, ea 63
Lesson 20 Long Vowel /ā/ai, ay 66
Lesson 21 Long Vowel /ā/a-e 69
Lesson 22 Long Vowel /ī/i-e 72
Lesson 23 Long Vowel /ō/o-e 75
Lesson 24 Consonants /s/c; /j/g, dge 78
Theme 5 Test 81

WATCH THIS!—BOOK 1-5

Lesson 25 Long Vowel /(y) o͞o/u-e 83
Lesson 26 Long Vowel /ī/y, ie, igh 86
Lesson 27 Vowel Diphthong /ou/ow, ou 89
Lesson 28 Long Vowel /ē/y, ie 92
Lesson 29 Vowel Variant /o͞o/oo, ew 95
Lesson 30 Long Vowels /ī/i, /ō/o 98
Theme 6 Test 101

Spelling Strategies 103
Word Sort Cards 104
Handwriting Models 105

Name _____

▶ **Read the Spelling Words. Then write each word in the group where it belongs.**

Words with <u>a</u>

_____
- - - - - - - - - - - - - - - - -
_____

_____

_____

_____

_____

_____

_____

_____   _____
- - - - - - - - - - - - - - - - -   - - - - - - - - - - - - - - - - -
_____   _____

_____

Word without <u>a</u>

_____
- - - - - - - - - - - - - - - - -
_____

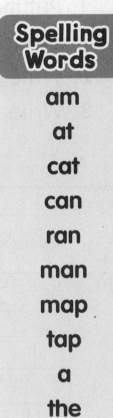

Spelling Words

am

at

cat

can

ran

man

map

tap

a

the

1

▶ **Make cards for the Spelling Words.**
Lay the cards down and read them.

1. Put the words with short <u>a</u> in one
group. Write the words on the chart.
2. Write the word with <u>e</u> on the chart.
3. Write the other word on the chart.

Spelling Words

am
at
cat
can
ran
man
map
tap
a
the

Words with Short <u>a</u>

_____   _____

----------------------   ----------------------

_____   _____

----------------------   ----------------------

_____   _____

----------------------   ----------------------

_____   _____

_____   _____

----------------------   ----------------------

_____   _____

Word with <u>e</u>	Other Word
_____	_____
--------------	--------------
_____	_____

2

Name _____

▶ **Write the letter or letters that complete each Spelling Word. Then trace and say each word.**

1. ___ m ___ n ___

2. ___ at ___

3. ___ m ___

4. ___ r ___ n ___

5. ___ c ___ n ___

6. ___ ta ___

7. ___ ma ___

8. _____

▶ **Unscramble the letters to make a Spelling Word.**

9. ta _____

10. eth _____

Spelling Practice Book
© Harcourt • Grade 1 • Book 1

Name _____

▶ **Read the Spelling Words. Then write each word in the group where it belongs.**

Words with <u>a</u>

_____   _____
- - - - - - - - - - -   - - - - - - - - - - -
_____   _____
- - - - - - - - - - -   - - - - - - - - - - -
_____   _____
- - - - - - - - - - -   - - - - - - - - - - -
_____   _____
- - - - - - - - - - -   - - - - - - - - - - -
_____   _____
- - - - - - - - - - -   - - - - - - - - - - -

Words without <u>a</u>

_____   _____
- - - - - - - - - - -   - - - - - - - - - - -
_____   _____

Spelling Words

hat

had

sad

sat

bat

bag

at

can

help

now

Spelling Practice Book
© Harcourt • Grade 1 • Book 1

Name _____

▶ **Make cards for the Spelling Words.
Lay the cards down and read them.**

1. Put the words with short <u>a</u> in one group. Write the words on the chart.
2. Write the word with <u>e</u> on the chart.
3. Write the word with <u>o</u> on the chart.

Spelling Words

hat
had
sad
sat
bat
bag
at
can
help
now

Words with Short <u>a</u>

Word with <u>e</u>	Word with <u>o</u>

Name _____

▶ **Unscramble the letters to make a Spelling Word.**

1. adh _____

2. atb _____

3. ats _____

4. ads _____

5. ta _____

6. gba _____

7. nca _____

8. tha _____

▶ **Write the letter that completes each Spelling Word. Then trace the rest of the word.**

9. 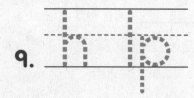 h lp

10. 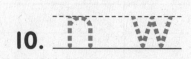 n w

Spelling Practice Book
© Harcourt • Grade 1 • Book 1

Name _____

▶ **Read the Spelling Words. Then write each word in the group where it belongs.**

Words with i

_____   _____
- - - - - - - - - - -   - - - - - - - - - - -
_____   _____
- - - - - - - - - - -   - - - - - - - - - - -
_____   _____
- - - - - - - - - - -   - - - - - - - - - - -
_____   _____

Words without i

_____   _____
- - - - - - - - - - -   - - - - - - - - - - -
_____   _____
- - - - - - - - - - -   - - - - - - - - - - -
_____   _____

Spelling Words

in
pin
pig
big
dig
did
had
sat
no
too

7

Name _____

▶ **Make cards for the Spelling Words.**
Lay the cards down and read them.

1. Put the words with short <u>i</u> in one
group. Write the words on the chart.

2. Put the words with <u>a</u> in one group.
Write the words on the chart.

3. Put the words with <u>o</u> in another
group. Write the words on the chart.

Spelling Words

in

pin

pig

big

dig

did

had

sat

no

too

Words with Short <u>i</u>

_____ _____

---------------------- ----------------------

_____ _____

---------------------- ----------------------

_____ _____

---------------------- ----------------------

_____ _____

Words with <u>a</u>	**Words with <u>o</u>**
_____	_____
------------	------------
_____	_____
------------	------------
_____	_____

8

Spelling Practice Book
© Harcourt • Grade 1 • Book 1

Name _____

▶ **Write the letter or letters that complete each Spelling Word. Then trace the rest of the word.**

1. i

2. t

3.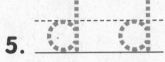

4.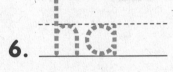

5.

6. ha

7. s t

8. n

▶ **Unscramble the letters to make a Spelling Word.**

9. npi _____

10. igb _____

Spelling Practice Book
© Harcourt • Grade 1 • Book 1

Name _____

▶ **Read each sentence. Look at how the two words are spelled. Fill in the circle next to the correct word.**

SAMPLE: The _____ naps.

       ○ kat   ● cat

1. They are _____.

     ○ sadd   ○ sad

2. Pam can _____.

     ○ help   ○ halp

3. Dad has a _____ van.

     ○ big   ○ bige

4. Will Max dig _____?

     ○ nuw   ○ now

5. We will fill a _____.

     ○ bag   ○ bagg

▶ **Read each pair of sentences. Look at how the underlined words are spelled. Then fill in the circle next to the correct sentence.**

SAMPLE: ● We have a <u>map</u>.

○ We have a <u>mapp</u>.

1. ○ I <u>did</u> not sit.

○ I <u>ded</u> not sit.

2. ○ I <u>em</u> big.

○ I <u>am</u> big.

3. ○ Sam sat on <u>the</u> mat.

○ Sam sat on <u>thu</u> mat.

4. ○ Pam has <u>noo</u> mat.

○ Pam has <u>no</u> mat.

5. ○ I can <u>tap</u>.

○ I can <u>tep</u>.

▶ **Read the Spelling Words. Then write each word in the group where it belongs.**

Words with <u>ck</u>

_____   _____

- - - - - - - - - - - - - - -   - - - - - - - - - - - - - - -

_____   _____

- - - - - - - - - - - - - - -   - - - - - - - - - - - - - - -

_____   _____

- - - - - - - - - - - - - - -   - - - - - - - - - - - - - - -

_____

Words without <u>ck</u>

_____   _____

- - - - - - - - - - - - - - -   - - - - - - - - - - - - - - -

_____   _____

- - - - - - - - - - - - - - -   - - - - - - - - - - - - - - -

_____

Spelling Words

pick
pack
tack
back
sack
sick
big
in
hold
so

Spelling Practice Book
© Harcourt • Grade 1 • Book 1

▶ **Make cards for the Spelling Words.**
Lay the cards down and read them.

1. Put the words with <u>a</u> in one group.
Write the words on the chart.

2. Put the words with <u>i</u> in one group.
Write the words on the chart.

3. Write the words with <u>o</u> on the chart.

Spelling Words

pick
pack
tack
back
sack
sick
big
in
hold
so

Words with <u>a</u>	Words with <u>i</u>

Words with <u>o</u>

_____ _____

13

Spelling Practice Book
© Harcourt • Grade 1 • Book 1

▶ **Write the letter or letters that complete each Spelling Word. Then trace the rest of the word.**

1. _____ i _____

2. _____ s _____

3. _____ b g _____

4. _____ h d _____

5. _____ pi _____

6. _____ sa _____

7. _____ t k _____

8. _____ b c _____

Spelling Words

pick
pack
tack
back
sack
sick
big
in
hold
so

▶ **Unscramble the letters to make a Spelling Word.**

9. ckpa _____

10. cski _____

▶ **Read the Spelling Words. Then write each word in the group where it belongs.**

Words with <u>o</u>

_____

_____   _____
- - - - - - - - -   - - - - - - - - -
_____   _____

_____   _____
- - - - - - - - -   - - - - - - - - -
_____   _____

_____   _____
- - - - - - - - -   - - - - - - - - -
_____   _____

_____
- - - - - - - - -
_____

Words without <u>o</u>

_____

_____   _____
- - - - - - - - -   - - - - - - - - -
_____   _____

_____
- - - - - - - - -
_____

Spelling Words

top
hop
hot
not
dot
lot
back
pick
oh
yes

Spelling Practice Book
© Harcourt • Grade 1 • Book 1

Name _____

▶ **Make cards for the Spelling Words.
Lay the cards down and read them.**

1. Put the words with short <u>o</u> in one
group. Write the words on the chart.

2. Write the other words on the chart.

Words with Short <u>o</u>

_____ _____

------------------------ ------------------------

_____ _____

------------------------ ------------------------

_____ _____

------------------------ ------------------------

_____ _____

------------------------ ------------------------

Other Words

_____ _____

------------------------ ------------------------

_____ _____

------------------------ ------------------------

Spelling Words

top

hop

hot

not

dot

lot

back

pick

oh

yes

Spelling Practice Book
© Harcourt • Grade 1 • Book 1

▶ **Write the letter or letters that complete each Spelling Word. Then trace and say each word.**

1. ___ 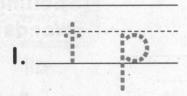 t p

2. ___ ba

3. ___ ot

4. ___ d t

5. ___ ye

6. ___ no

7. ___ h p

8. ___ o

Spelling Words

top
hop
hot
not
dot
lot
back
pick
oh
yes

▶ **Unscramble the letters to make a Spelling Word.**

9. cipk ___

___

10. oth ___

___

Spelling Practice Book
© Harcourt • Grade 1 • Book 1

Name ______________________________

Read the Spelling Words. Then write each word in the group where it belongs.

Spelling Words

- all
- call
- fall
- wall
- ball
- tall
- not
- top
- much
- thank

Words with all

______________ ______________

______________ ______________

______________ ______________

______________ ______________

Words without all

______________ ______________

______________ ______________

______________ ______________

▶ **Make cards for the Spelling Words.**
Lay the cards down and read them.

1. Put the words with <u>all</u> in one group.
   Write the words on the chart.
2. Put the words with short <u>o</u> in one
   group. Write the words on the chart.
3. Write the other words on the chart.

Spelling Words

all
call
fall
wall
ball
tall
not
top
much
thank

Words with <u>all</u>

_____   _____

_____   _____

_____   _____

_____   _____

_____

Words with Short <u>o</u>	Other Words
_____	_____
_____	_____
_____	_____

Name _____

▶ **Write the letter or letters that complete each Spelling Word. Then trace the rest of the word.**

1. _____ al _____

2. _____ t ll _____

3. _____ th _ k _____

4. _____ mu _____

5. _____ b ll _____

6. _____ wa _____

7. _____ n t _____

8. _____ t p _____

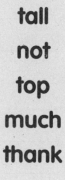

Spelling Words

all
call
fall
wall
ball
tall
not
top
much
thank

▶ **Unscramble the letters to make a Spelling Word.**

9. lalc

_____

- - - - - - - - - - -

_____

10. alfl

_____

- - - - - - - - - - -

_____

Spelling Practice Book
© Harcourt • Grade 1 • Book 1

► **Read each sentence. Look at how the two words are spelled. Fill in the circle next to the correct word.**

SAMPLE: Dad has a _____.

      ○ het   ● hat

1. A cat sits on the _____.

     ○ wall   ○ wol

2. An ant is in the _____.

     ○ sak   ○ sack

3. Can you _____ my bag?

     ○ hald   ○ hold

4. The pig is _____ too big.

     ○ mech   ○ much

5. It is on _____ of the box.

     ○ top   ○ topp

Spelling Practice Book
© Harcourt • Grade 1 • Book 1

Name _____

▶ **Read each pair of sentences. Look at how the underlined words are spelled. Then fill in the circle next to the correct sentence.**

SAMPLE: ○ Dad did not <u>pac</u> a ball.
● Dad did not <u>pack</u> a ball.

1. ○ I will <u>thenk</u> Mom.
   ○ I will <u>thank</u> Mom.

2. ○ She is <u>tahl</u>.
   ○ She is <u>tall</u>.

3. ○ My dog can dig a <u>lott</u>.
   ○ My dog can dig a <u>lot</u>.

4. ○ I am <u>sick</u>.
   ○ I am <u>sik</u>.

5. ○ We will come <u>back</u>.
   ○ We will come <u>bak</u>.

Spelling Practice Book
© Harcourt • Grade 1 • Book 1

Name _____

▶ **Read the Spelling Words. Then write each word in the group where it belongs.**

Words with e

_____   _____

_____   _____

_____   _____

_____   _____

_____   _____

_____

Words without e

_____

_____

_____

_____

_____

23

▶ **Make cards for the Spelling Words.**
Lay the cards down and read them.

1. Put the words with short <u>e</u> in one group. Write the words on the chart.
2. Put the words that rhyme with <u>ball</u> in one group. Write them on the chart.
3. Write the other words on the chart.

set
sent
ten
tell
let
get
all
call
make
of

Words with Short <u>e</u>

_____   _____

_____   _____

_____   _____

_____   _____

_____   _____

_____   _____

Words That Rhyme with <u>ball</u>

_____   _____

_____   _____

Other Words

_____   _____

_____   _____

_____

Name _____

▶ **Unscramble the letters to write a Spelling Word.**

1. kema

_____

- - - - - - - - - - - - - - - - - - -

_____

2. etns

_____

- - - - - - - - - - - - - - - - - - -

_____

3. lal

_____

- - - - - - - - - - - - - - - - - - -

_____

4. ent

_____

- - - - - - - - - - - - - - - - - - -

_____

5. lelt

_____

- - - - - - - - - - - - - - - - - - -

_____

6. est

_____

- - - - - - - - - - - - - - - - - - -

_____

7. lcla

_____

- - - - - - - - - - - - - - - - - - -

_____

8. lte

_____

- - - - - - - - - - - - - - - - - - -

_____

Spelling Words

set

sent

ten

tell

let

get

all

call

make

of

▶ **Write the letter or letters that complete each Spelling Word.**

9. g_____

_____

- - - - - - - - - - - - - - - - - - -

10. _____f

_____

- - - - - - - - - - - - - - - - - - -

Spelling Practice Book
© Harcourt • Grade 1 • Book 2

▶ **Read the Spelling Words. Then write each word in the group where it belongs.**

Words with <u>th</u>

_____   _____

_____   _____

_____   _____

_____   _____

_____   _____

Words without <u>th</u>

_____   _____

_____   _____

_____   _____

Spelling Words

then

them

this

that

path

with

ten

get

said

was

Spelling Practice Book
© Harcourt • Grade 1 • Book 2

Name _____

▶ **Make cards for the Spelling Words.
Lay the cards down and read them.**

1. Put the words with <u>e</u> in one group.
Write the words on the chart.

2. Put the words with <u>a</u> in one group.
Write the words on the chart.

3. Write the other words on the chart.

Spelling Words

then
them
this
that
path
with
ten
get
said
was

Words with <u>e</u>	Words with <u>a</u>
_____	_____
_____	_____
_____	_____
_____	_____
_____	_____
_____	_____
_____	

Other Words

_____	_____
_____	_____

Spelling Practice Book
© Harcourt • Grade 1 • Book 2

Name _____

► **Write the letter or letters that complete each Spelling Word. Then trace the rest of the word.**

1. w_____s

w s

2. th_____n

th n

3. wi_____

wi

4. t_____n

t n

5. s_____d

s d

6. g_____

g

7. _____is

is

8. th_____

th

► **Unscramble the letters to make a Spelling Word.**

9. emth

_____

10. thpa

_____

Spelling Practice Book
© Harcourt • Grade 1 • Book 2

▶ **Read the Spelling Words. Then write each word in the group where it belongs.**

Words with <u>u</u>

_____   _____

----------------------   ----------------------

_____   _____

----------------------   ----------------------

_____   _____

----------------------   ----------------------

_____   _____

Words without <u>u</u>

_____   _____

----------------------   ----------------------

_____   _____

----------------------   ----------------------

Spelling Words

us

bus

must

cut

cub

club

with

then

don't

says

Spelling Practice Book
© Harcourt • Grade 1 • Book 2

Name _____

Name _____

Name _____

Name _____

Name _____

Short Vowel /u/u

Lesson 9

▶ **Make cards for the Spelling Words.
Lay the cards down and read them.**

1. Put the words with <u>us</u> in one group.
   Put the words with <u>ub</u> in another
   group. Write the words on the chart.
2. Write the other words on the chart.

Spelling Words

us
bus
must
cut
cub
club
with
then
don't
says

Words with <u>us</u>	Words with <u>ub</u>
_____	_____
_____	_____
_____	_____
_____	

Other Words

_____	_____
_____	_____
_____	

30

Spelling Practice Book
© Harcourt • Grade 1 • Book 2

Name _____

▶ **Write the letter or letters that complete each Spelling Word. Then trace the rest of the word.**

Spelling
Words

us
bus
must
cut
cub
club
with
then
don't
says

1. _____s

2. b_____s

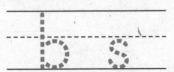

3. cl_____

4. c_____t

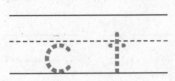

5. mu_____

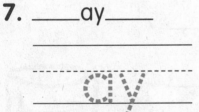

6. c_____b

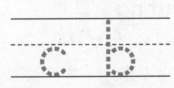

7. _____ay_____

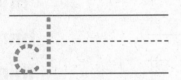

8. d_____'t

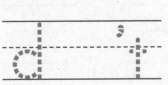

▶ **Unscramble the letters to make a Spelling Word.**

9. thiw

_____

10. neth

_____

31

▶ **Read the Spelling Words. Then write each word in the group where it belongs.**

Words with ng

_____   _____
- - - - - - - - - - - - - - -   - - - - - - - - - - - - - - -

_____   _____
- - - - - - - - - - - - - - -   - - - - - - - - - - - - - - -

_____   _____
- - - - - - - - - - - - - - -   - - - - - - - - - - - - - - -

_____   _____

Words without ng

_____   _____
- - - - - - - - - - - - - - -   - - - - - - - - - - - - - - -

_____   _____

_____   _____
- - - - - - - - - - - - - - -   - - - - - - - - - - - - - - -

_____   _____

Spelling Words

long
song
sing
ring
bring
thing
us
must
does
food

▶ **Make cards for the Spelling Words.**
Lay the cards down and read them.

1. Put the words with <u>ing</u> in one group.
Write the words on the chart.

2. Write the other words on the chart.

Words with <u>ing</u>

_____   _____

- - - - - - - - - - - - - - -   - - - - - - - - - - - - - - -

_____   _____

- - - - - - - - - - - - - - -   - - - - - - - - - - - - - - -

_____   _____

Other Words

_____   _____

- - - - - - - - - - - - - - -   - - - - - - - - - - - - - - -

_____   _____

- - - - - - - - - - - - - - -   - - - - - - - - - - - - - - -

_____   _____

Name _____

▶ **Write the letter or letters that complete each Spelling Word. Then trace the rest of the word.**

1. mu_____

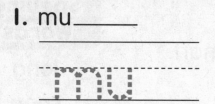

2. s_____ng

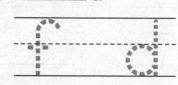

3. _____s

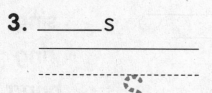

4. f_____d

5. lo_____

6. _____oe_____

Spelling Words

long
song
sing
ring
bring
thing
us
must
does
food

▶ **Write four Spelling Words that rhyme with <u>king</u>.**

7. _____

8. _____

9. _____

10. _____

Spelling Practice Book
© Harcourt • Grade 1 • Book 2

▶ **Read the Spelling Words. Then write each word in the group where it belongs.**

Words with <u>or</u>

_____   _____

_____   _____

_____   _____

_____   _____

_____   _____

Words without <u>or</u>

_____   _____

_____   _____

_____   _____

Spelling Words

or
for
form
more
store
sort
long
bring
your
head

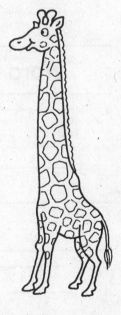

Spelling Practice Book
© Harcourt • Grade 1 • Book 2

▶ **Make cards for the Spelling Words.
Lay the cards down and read them.**

1. Put the words with <u>or</u> in one group.
   Write the words on the chart.
2. Find the word with <u>ou</u> and the word
   with <u>ea</u>. Write the words on the chart.
3. Write the words with <u>ng</u> on the chart.

Words with <u>or</u>

_____   _____

_____   _____

_____   _____

_____   _____

_____   _____

Word with <u>ou</u>	Word with <u>ea</u>
_____	_____
_____	_____

Words with <u>ng</u>

_____   _____

_____   _____

Spelling Practice Book
© Harcourt • Grade 1 • Book 2

Name _____

▶ **Write the letter or letters that complete each Spelling Word. Then trace the rest of the word.**

1. f____r
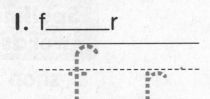

2. lo____
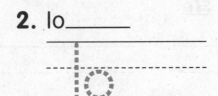

3. ____r
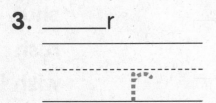

4. m____r____
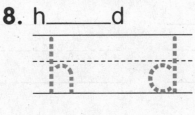

5. fo____
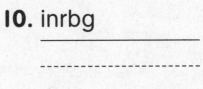

6. st____e

7. y____r

8. h____d

▶ **Unscramble the letters to write a Spelling Word.**

9. rtso
_____

10. inrbg
_____

37

Name _____

▶ **Read the Spelling Words. Then write each word in the group where it belongs.**

Words with <u>sh</u>

_____ _____

_____ _____

_____ _____

_____ _____

Spelling Words

shop

shot

shut

rush

wish

fish

for

more

from

very

Words without <u>sh</u>

_____ _____

_____ _____

_____ _____

38

Spelling Practice Book
© Harcourt • Grade 1 • Book 2

▶ **Make cards for the Spelling Words.**
Lay the cards down and read them.

Spelling Words

shop
shot
shut
rush
wish
fish
for
more
from
very

1. Put words that begin with <u>sh</u> in
one group and words that end with <u>sh</u>
in another. Write them on the chart.
2. Write the other words on the chart.

Begin with <u>sh</u>	End with <u>sh</u>
_____	_____
_____	_____
_____	_____
_____	_____
_____	_____

Other Words

_____   _____
_____   _____
_____   _____

Spelling Practice Book
© Harcourt • Grade 1 • Book 2

Name _____

▶ **Write the letter or letters that complete each Spelling Word. Then trace the rest of the word.**

1. sh_____p

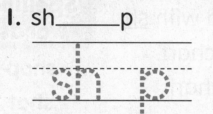

2. ru_____

3. _____ot

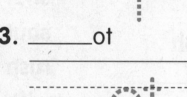

4. fr_____m

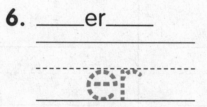

5. _____ut

6. _____er_____

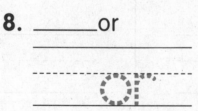

7. mor_____

8. _____or

▶ **Write two Spelling Words that rhyme with <u>dish</u>.**

9. _____

10. _____

Spelling Practice Book
© Harcourt • Grade 1 • Book 2

Name _____

▶ **Read each sentence. Look at how the two words are spelled. Fill in the circle next to the correct word.**

SAMPLE: We got on the _____.

     ○ bis   ● bus

1. We will _____ for a dress.

   ○ shep   ○ shop

2. Here is a good _____.

   ○ store   ○ storr

3. Will you _____ me a gift?

   ○ bring   ○ breng

4. Dad will get _____.

   ○ fud   ○ food

5. _____ him what you like.

   ○ Tel   ○ Tell

41

▶ **Read each pair of sentences. Look at how the underlined words are spelled. Then fill in the circle next to the correct sentence.**

SAMPLE: ○ <u>Den't</u> drop the dish.
● <u>Don't</u> drop the dish.

1. ○ Mom <u>musst</u> cut the ham.
○ Mom <u>must</u> cut the ham.

2. ○ <u>This</u> one is the best.
○ <u>Thes</u> one is the best.

3. ○ We can have it <u>with</u> milk.
○ We can have it <u>weth</u> milk.

4. ○ Miss North <u>sent</u> some corn.
○ Miss North <u>sint</u> some corn.

5. ○ I <u>wis</u> we had more milk.
○ I <u>wish</u> we had more milk.

Spelling Practice Book
© Harcourt • Grade 1 • Book 2

Name _____

▶ **Read the Spelling Words. Then write each word in the group where it belongs.**

Words with ch

_____   _____
_____   _____

_____   _____
_____   _____

_____   _____
_____   _____

Words without ch

_____   _____
_____   _____

_____   _____
_____   _____

Spelling Words

chip
chin
inch
such
catch
match
wish
shop
saw
were

Spelling Practice Book
© Harcourt • Grade 1 • Book 3

▶ **Make cards for the Spelling Words.**
Lay the cards down and read them.

1. Put the words with <u>ch</u> in one group.
   Write the words on the chart. Circle
   the words that have a <u>t</u>.
2. Write the other words on the chart.

Spelling Words

chip

chin

inch

such

catch

match

wish

shop

saw

were

Words with <u>ch</u>

_____   _____

_____   _____

_____   _____

_____   _____

Other Words

_____   _____

_____   _____

_____   _____

Spelling Practice Book
© Harcourt • Grade 1 • Book 3

Name _____

▶ **Write the letter or letters that complete each Spelling Word. Then trace the rest of the word.**

1. su_____

   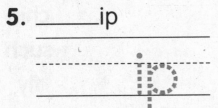

2. wi_____

3. ch_____n

   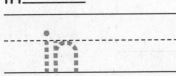

4. sh_____

   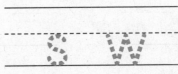

5. _____ip

6. wer_____

7. in_____

8. s_____w

Spelling Words

chip
chin
inch
such
catch
match
wish
shop
saw
were

▶ **Write two Spelling Words that rhyme with patch.**

9. _____

10. _____

45

Spelling Practice Book
© Harcourt • Grade 1 • Book 3

Name _____

▶ **Read the Spelling Words. Then write each word in the group where it belongs.**

Words with <u>ar</u>

_____   _____

_____   _____

_____   _____

_____   _____

Words without <u>ar</u>

_____   _____

_____   _____

Spelling Words

far
farm
arm
art
part
park
chin
such
fly
watch

Spelling Practice Book
© Harcourt • Grade 1 • Book 3

▶ **Make cards for the Spelling Words.
Lay the cards down and read them.**

I. Put words with <u>ar</u> in one group. Put
   words with <u>ch</u> in another group. Write
   the words on the chart.

2. Write the word with <u>y</u> on the chart.

**Spelling
Words**

far
farm
arm
art
part
park
chin
such
fly
watch

Words with <u>ar</u>

_____   _____

_____   _____

_____   _____

_____   _____

_____   _____

Words with <u>ch</u>   Word with <u>y</u>

_____   _____

_____

_____

_____

▶ **Write the letter or letters that complete each Spelling Word. Then trace the rest of the word.**

1. ___rt
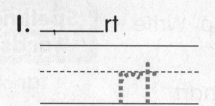

2. p___t
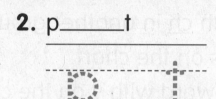

3. a___m
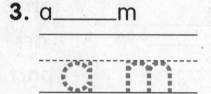

4. f___r
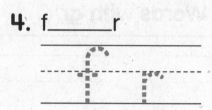

5. ___rk
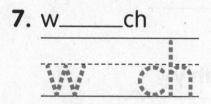

6. su___
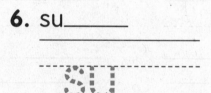

7. w___ch

8. fl___

▶ **Unscramble the letters to make a Spelling Word.**

9. afmr _____

10. hcni _____

Spelling Practice Book
© Harcourt • Grade 1 • Book 3

▶ **Read the Spelling Words. Then write each word in the group where it belongs.**

Words with <u>wh</u>

_____   _____
- - - - - - - - - - - - - - - -   - - - - - - - - - - - - - - - -
_____   _____
- - - - - - - - - - - - - - - -
_____

**Spelling
Words**

quit

quick

quiz

whiz

which

when

arm

part

house

put

Words with <u>qu</u>

_____   _____
- - - - - - - - - - - - - - - -   - - - - - - - - - - - - - - - -
_____   _____
- - - - - - - - - - - - - - - -

Other Words

_____   _____
- - - - - - - - - - - - - - - -   - - - - - - - - - - - - - - - -
_____   _____
- - - - - - - - - - - - - - - -   - - - - - - - - - - - - - - - -
_____   _____

▶ **Make cards for the Spelling Words.**
Lay the cards down and read them.

1. Put words with <u>qu</u> in a group.
Put words with <u>wh</u> in another group.
Put words with <u>ar</u> in a third group.
Write the words on the chart.

2. Write the other words on the chart.

Spelling Words

quit
quick
quiz
whiz
which
when
arm
part
house
put

Words with <u>qu</u>	Words with <u>wh</u>
_____	_____
_____	_____
_____	_____
_____	_____

Words with <u>ar</u>	Other Words
_____	_____
_____	_____
_____	_____

Spelling Practice Book
© Harcourt • Grade 1 • Book 3

▶ **Unscramble the letters to write a Spelling Word.**

1. iqkcu

_____

- - - - - - - - - - - -

_____

2. tiqu

_____

- - - - - - - - - - - -

_____

3. zwhi

_____

- - - - - - - - - - - -

_____

4. chhiw

_____

- - - - - - - - - - - -

_____

5. mra

_____

- - - - - - - - - - - -

_____

6. newh

_____

- - - - - - - - - - - -

_____

7. atrp

_____

- - - - - - - - - - - -

_____

8. iqzu

_____

- - - - - - - - - - - -

_____

Spelling Words

quit
quick
quiz
whiz
which
when
arm
part
house
put

▶ **Write the letter or letters that complete each Spelling Word. Then trace the rest of the word.**

9. h____se

10. ____u____

51

Spelling Practice Book
© Harcourt • Grade 1 • Book 3

▶ **Read the Spelling Words. Then write each word in the group where it belongs.**

Words with r

_____   _____

-    -

_____   _____

_____   _____

-    -

_____   _____

_____   _____

-    -

_____   _____

_____

- -

_____

Spelling Words

her
fur
turn
bird
girl
first
quit
when
name
work

Words without r

_____

- -

_____   _____

- -

_____

- -

_____

Name _____

▶ **Make cards for the Spelling Words.**
Lay the cards down and read them.

1. Put the words with <u>ur</u> in one group.
Put the words with <u>ir</u> in another group.
Write the words on the chart.

2. Write the other words on the chart.

Spelling Words

her
fur
turn
bird
girl
first
quit
when
name
work

Words with <u>ur</u>	Words with <u>ir</u>
_____	_____
_____	_____
_____	_____
	_____

Other Words

_____   _____

_____   _____

_____   _____

_____

Spelling Practice Book
© Harcourt • Grade 1 • Book 3

Name _____

r-Controlled vowels
/ûr/ er, ir, ur
Lesson 16

▶ **Write the letter or letters that complete each Spelling Word. Then trace the rest of the word.**

1. gi____l

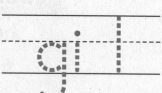

2. ____er

3. wh____n

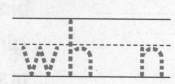

4. w____rk

5. f____r

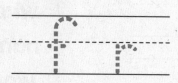

6. nam____

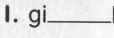

7. q____t

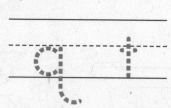

8. b____d

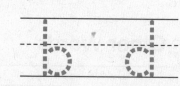

▶ **Unscramble the letters to make a Spelling Word.**

9. trfsi

_____

10. utnr

_____

Name _____

▶ **Read the Spelling Words. Then write each word in the group where it belongs.**

Words with le

_____

_____

_____

_____

Words without le

_____

_____

_____

_____

Spelling Words

hand

handle

wig

wiggle

single

little

turn

girl

by

room

Spelling Practice Book
© Harcourt • Grade 1 • Book 3

▶ **Make çards for the Spelling Words.**
Lay the cards down and read them.

1. Put the words with <u>i</u> in a group. Put the words with <u>a</u> in another group. Write the words on the chart. Circle the words with <u>le</u>.

2. Write the other words on the chart.

Words with <u>i</u>	Words with <u>a</u>
_____	_____
- - - - - - - - -	- - - - - - - - -
_____	_____
- - - - - - - - -	- - - - - - - - -
_____	_____
- - - - - - - - -	**Other Words**
_____	_____
- - - - - - - - -	- - - - - - - - -
_____	_____
- - - - - - - - -	_____
_____	- - - - - - - - -
- - - - - - - - -	_____
_____	- - - - - - - - -

Spelling Words

hand
handle
wig
wiggle
single
little
turn
girl
by
room

Spelling Practice Book
© Harcourt • Grade 1 • Book 3

Name _____

▶ **Write the letter or letters that complete each Spelling Word. Then trace the rest of the word.**

1. b_____
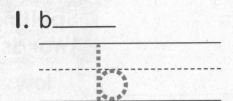

2. wi_____le
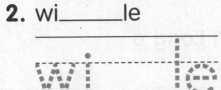

3. t_____n
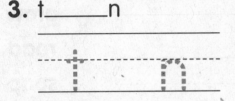

4. g_____l
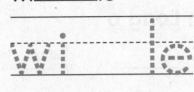

5. r_____m

6. lit_____
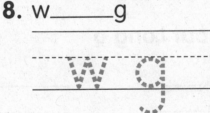

7. s_____gle
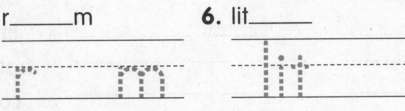

8. w_____g

9. h_____d

▶ **Write the Spelling Word that rhymes with <u>sandal</u>.**

_____

10. _____

▶ **Read the Spelling Words. Then write each word in the group where it belongs.**

Words with Long o

_____   _____

- - - - - - - - - - - - - -   - - - - - - - - - - - - - -

_____   _____

- - - - - - - - - - - - - -   - - - - - - - - - - - - - -

_____   _____

- - - - - - - - - - - - - -   - - - - - - - - - - - - - -

_____   _____

- - - - - - - - - - - - - -   - - - - - - - - - - - - - -

Words without Long o

_____   _____

- - - - - - - - - - - - - -   - - - - - - - - - - - - - -

_____   _____

- - - - - - - - - - - - - -   - - - - - - - - - - - - - -

Spelling Words
low
slow
grow
road
soap
boat
little
handle
carry
would

Spelling Practice Book
© Harcourt • Grade 1 • Book 3

Name _____

▶ **Make cards for the Spelling Words.
Lay the cards down and read them.**

1. Put the words with <u>ow</u> in a group. Put the words with <u>oa</u> in another group. Put the words with <u>le</u> in a third group. Write the words on the chart.

2. Write the other words on the chart.

Spelling Words

low
slow
grow
road
soap
boat
little
handle
carry
would

Words with <u>ow</u>	Words with <u>oa</u>
_____	_____
_____	_____
_____	_____
_____	_____

Words with <u>le</u>	Other Words
_____	_____
_____	_____
_____	_____

▶ **Write the letter or letters that complete each Spelling Word. Then trace the rest of the word.**

1. s____p
   s____p

2. car____
   car

3. li____le
   li__le

4. ro____
   ro

5. w____ld
   w__ld

6. hand____
   hand

7. b____t
   b__t

8. lo____
   lo

▶ **Write the two Spelling Words that rhyme with low.**

9. _____

10. _____

Spelling Practice Book
© Harcourt • Grade 1 • Book 3

► **Read each sentence. Look at how the two words are spelled. Fill in the circle next to the correct word.**

SAMPLE: The plant will _____ tall.

  ○ gro   ● grow

1. Bob can _____ the pot.

   ○ kerry   ○ carry

2. A little _____ sits on a branch.

   ○ bird   ○ burd

3. Fran fell on her _____.

   ○ cin   ○ chin

4. They have a big _____.

   ○ farm   ○ ferm

5. _____ pig is bigger?

   ○ Quich   ○ Which

Name _____

▶ **Read each pair of sentences. Look at how the underlined words are spelled. Then fill in the circle next to the correct sentence.**

SAMPLE: ● Turn the <u>little</u> red car.
○ Turn the <u>litel</u> red car.

I. ○ She turns the <u>handal</u>.
○ She turns the <u>handle</u>.

2. ○ Don't <u>quit</u> yet.
○ Don't <u>qiut</u> yet.

3. ○ I will <u>catch</u> up to you.
○ I will <u>cach</u> up to you.

4. ○ This is the fun <u>pert</u>.
○ This is the fun <u>part</u>.

5. ○ Let's paddle the <u>bowt</u>.
○ Let's paddle the <u>boat</u>.

Name _____

▶ **Read the Spelling Words. Then write each word in the group where it belongs.**

Words with Long e

_____

_____

_____

_____

_____

_____

_____

_____

Words without Long e

_____

_____

_____

_____

_____

_____

> ## Spelling Words
>
> me
> see
> feet
> seat
> mean
> team
> slow
> road
> our
> over

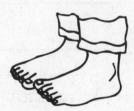

63

Spelling Practice Book
© Harcourt • Grade 1 • Book 4

Name _____

▶ **Make cards for the Spelling Words. Lay the cards down and read them.**

1. Put the words with long <u>e</u> in one group. Write the words on the chart. Circle the letters that make long <u>e</u>.

2. Write the other words on the chart.

Words with Long <u>e</u>

_____   _____
---------------------   ---------------------
_____   _____
---------------------   ---------------------
_____   _____
---------------------   ---------------------

Other Words

_____   _____
---------------------   ---------------------
_____   _____
---------------------   ---------------------

Spelling Words

me
see
feet
seat
mean
team
slow
road
our
over

Spelling Practice Book
© Harcourt • Grade 1 • Book 4

Name _____

▶ **Write the letter or letters that complete each Spelling Word. Then trace and say each word.**

1. m _____

2. f _____

3. m _ n

4. s t _____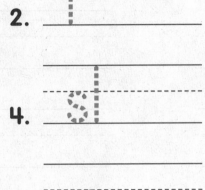

5. t _ m

6. o _____

7. r _ d

8. s _ t

Spelling Words

me

see

feet

seat

mean

team

slow

road

our

over

▶ **Unscramble the letters to make a Spelling Word.**

9. rvoe _____

10. ese _____

Spelling Practice Book
© Harcourt • Grade 1 • Book 4

Name _____

▶ **Read the Spelling Words. Then write each word in the group where it belongs.**

Words with Long <u>a</u>

_____   _____
- - - - - - - - - -   - - - - - - - - - -
_____   _____

_____   _____
- - - - - - - - - -   - - - - - - - - - -
_____   _____

_____   _____
- - - - - - - - - -   - - - - - - - - - -

Words without Long <u>a</u>

_____   _____
- - - - - - - - - -   - - - - - - - - - -
_____   _____

_____   _____
- - - - - - - - - -   - - - - - - - - - -

Spelling Words

day
say
play
plain
rain
wait
feet
me
door
told

Spelling Practice Book
© Harcourt • Grade 1 • Book 4

Name _____

noqa

▶ **Make cards for the Spelling Words. Lay the cards down and read them.**

1. Put the words with <u>ay</u> in one group. Put the words with <u>ai</u> in another group. Write the words on the chart.
2. Write the other words on the chart.

Spelling Words

day
say
play
plain
rain
wait
feet
me
door
told

Words with <u>ay</u>	Words with <u>ai</u>

Other Words

67

Name _____

▶ **Write the letter or letters that complete each Spelling Word. Then trace the rest of the word.**

1. f___t

2. pl___

3. p___in

4. r___n

5. s___y

6. d___r

7. t___d

8. ___m

Spelling Words

day
say
play
plain
rain
wait
feet
me
door
told

▶ **Unscramble the letters to make a Spelling Word.**

9. yda

_____

10. tiwa

_____

68

Name _____

▶ **Read the Spelling Words. Then write each word in the group where it belongs.**

Words with Long <u>a</u>

came

game

gate

late

lake

take

day

play

four

place

_____   _____
-----------------------   -----------------------
_____   _____

_____   _____
-----------------------   -----------------------
_____   _____

_____   _____
-----------------------   -----------------------
_____   _____

_____   _____
-----------------------   -----------------------
_____   _____

_____

_____

Word without Long <u>a</u>

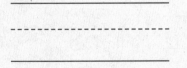

_____

_____

69

Spelling Practice Book
© Harcourt • Grade 1 • Book 4

Name _____

▶ **Make cards for the Spelling Words.**
Lay the cards down and read them.

1. Put the words with long <u>a</u> and silent <u>e</u> in one group. Write the words on the chart.

2. Write the other words on the chart.

Words with Long <u>a</u> and Silent <u>e</u>

_____   _____

_____   _____

_____   _____

_____   _____

_____   _____

_____

Other Words

_____   _____

_____   _____

_____

Name _____

▶ **Write the letter or letters that complete each Spelling Word. Then trace the rest of the word.**

1. _____ gat _____

2. _____ pla e _____

3. _____ t _____

4. _____ g m _____

5. _____ f r _____

6. _____ c _____

Spelling Words

came
game
gate
late
lake
take
day
play
four
place

▶ **Write two Spelling Words that rhyme with <u>cake</u>.**

7. _____

8. _____

▶ **Write two Spelling Words that rhyme with <u>hay</u>.**

9. _____

10. _____

Spelling Practice Book
© Harcourt • Grade 1 • Book 4

Name _____

▶ **Read the Spelling Words. Then write each word in the group where it belongs.**

Words with Long i

_____   _____

_____   _____

_____   _____

_____   _____

_____   _____

Words without Long i

_____   _____

_____   _____

_____   _____

Spelling Words

like

line

nine

mine

mile

while

take

came

gone

near

Spelling Practice Book
© Harcourt • Grade 1 • Book 4

▶ **Make cards for the Spelling Words. Lay the cards down and read them.**

1. Put the words with long <u>i</u> and silent <u>e</u> in a group. Write the words on the chart.

2. Write the other words on the chart.

Words with Long <u>i</u> and Silent <u>e</u>

_____   _____

_____   _____

_____   _____

_____   _____

_____   _____

Other Words

_____   _____

_____   _____

_____   _____

Spelling Words

like
line
nine
mine
mile
while
take
came
gone
near

Name _____

▶ **Unscramble the letters to write a Spelling Word.**

1. engo
_____
- - - - - - - - - - - - -
_____

2. ilewh
_____
- - - - - - - - - - - - -
_____

3. keli
_____
- - - - - - - - - - - - -
_____

4. ceam
_____
- - - - - - - - - - - - -
_____

5. iemn
_____
- - - - - - - - - - - - -
_____

6. keta
_____
- - - - - - - - - - - - -
_____

7. nien
_____
- - - - - - - - - - - - -
_____

8. miel
_____
- - - - - - - - - - - - -
_____

Spelling Words

like
line
nine
mine
mile
while
take
came
gone
near

▶ **Write the letter or letters that complete each Spelling Word.**

9. _____ i _(e)_ _____

10. _____ n r _____

▶ **Read the Spelling Words. Then write each word in the group where it belongs.**

Words with Long <u>o</u>

_____   _____

_____   _____

_____   _____

_____   _____

_____   _____

Words without Long <u>o</u>

_____   _____

_____   _____

Spelling Words

home

hope

rope

rode

rose

those

like

nine

right

walk

Spelling Practice Book
© Harcourt • Grade 1 • Book 4

Name _____

▶ **Make cards for the Spelling Words.**
Lay the cards down and read them.

1. Put the words with long <u>o</u> and silent <u>e</u>
in one group. Write the words on the
chart.

2. Write the other words on the chart.

Words with Long <u>o</u> and Silent <u>e</u>

_____   _____

_____   _____

_____   _____

_____   _____

_____   _____

Other Words

_____   _____

_____   _____

_____   _____

Spelling Practice Book
© Harcourt • Grade 1 • Book 4

Name _____

▶ **Write the letter or letters that complete each Spelling Word. Then trace the rest of the word.**

1. ___ rod

2. ___ nin

3. ___ h ___ p

4. ___ w ___ lk

5. ___ h ___ e

6. ___ ri ___ t

7. ___ rop

8. ___ lk

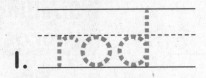

Spelling Words

home
hope
rope
rode
rose
those
like
nine
right
walk

▶ **Write two Spelling Words that rhyme with <u>nose</u>.**

9. _____

10. _____

Spelling Practice Book
© Harcourt • Grade 1 • Book 4

Name _____

Consonants /s/c;
/j/g, dge
Lesson 24

▶ **Read the Spelling Words. Then write each word in the group where it belongs.**

Words with <u>c</u>

_____   _____

- - - - - - - - - - - - - -   - - - - - - - - - - - - - -

_____   _____

- - - - - - - - - - - - - -

_____

Words with <u>g</u>

_____   _____

- - - - - - - - - - - - - -   - - - - - - - - - - - - - -

_____   _____

_____

- - - - - - - - - - - - - -

_____

Words without <u>c</u> or <u>g</u>

_____   _____

- - - - - - - - - - - - - -   - - - - - - - - - - - - - -

_____   _____

_____   _____

- - - - - - - - - - - - - -   - - - - - - - - - - - - - -

_____   _____

Spelling Words

ice
nice
race
page
edge
large
home
those
love
hello

Consonants /s/c;
/j/g, dge
Lesson 24

Name _____

▶ **Make cards for the Spelling Words.**
Lay the cards down and read them.

1. Put the words with a long vowel and
   silent <u>e</u> in one group. Write the words
   on the chart.
2. Write the other words on the chart.

Words with Long Vowel and Silent <u>e</u>

_____

_____   _____

_____   _____

_____   _____

_____   _____

Other Words

_____

_____   _____

_____   _____

Spelling Practice Book
© Harcourt • Grade 1 • Book 4

▶ **Write the letter or letters that complete each Spelling Word. Then trace the rest of the word.**

1. e ge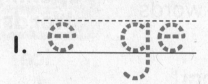

2. h me

3. ra

4. tho

5. he lo

6. i e

▶ **Unscramble the letters to make a Spelling Word**

7. gepa _____

8. raelg _____

▶ **Write two Spelling Words that rhyme with <u>dice</u>.**

9. _____

10. _____

80

Spelling Practice Book
© Harcourt • Grade 1 • Book 4

▶ **Read each sentence. Look at how the two words are spelled. Fill in the circle next to the correct word.**

SAMPLE: I _____ we go to the park.

⚪ hoap   ⬤ hope

1. All the girls like to _____.

   ⚪ rase   ⚪ race

2. They _____ their bikes to the park.

   ⚪ rode   ⚪ rowd

3. Can we _____ the riddle game?

   ⚪ plae   ⚪ play

4. The red _____ can go first.

   ⚪ teme   ⚪ team

5. Don't be ____!

   ⚪ late   ⚪ layt

Name _____

▶ **Read each pair of sentences. Look at how the underlined words are spelled. Then fill in the circle next to the correct sentence.**

SAMPLE: ○ There are <u>nin</u> bikes.
⬤ There are <u>nine</u> bikes.

1. ○ Can you <u>see</u> the forest?
   ○ Can you <u>se</u> the forest?

2. ○ The <u>rayn</u> made the tent wet.
   ○ The <u>rain</u> made the tent wet.

3. ○ We will <u>wolk</u> on the path.
   ○ We will <u>walk</u> on the path.

4. ○ The path is one <u>mile</u> long.
   ○ The path is one <u>mil</u> long.

5. ○ We sit on the <u>edge</u> of it.
   ○ We sit on the <u>edje</u> of it.

Spelling Practice Book
© Harcourt • Grade 1 • Book 4

Name _____

▶ **Read the Spelling Words. Then write each word in the group where it belongs.**

Words with u

_____   _____
- - - - - - - - - -   - - - - - - - - - -
_____   _____

_____   _____
- - - - - - - - - -   - - - - - - - - - -
_____   _____

_____   _____
- - - - - - - - - -   - - - - - - - - - -
_____   _____

Words without u

_____   _____
- - - - - - - - - -   - - - - - - - - - -
_____   _____

_____   _____
- - - - - - - - - -   - - - - - - - - - -
_____   _____

Spelling Words

use
cute
cube
tube
tune
rule
nice
large
hear
talk

Spelling Practice Book
© Harcourt • Grade 1 • Book 5

▶ **Make cards for the Spelling Words.**
Lay the cards down and read them.

1. Put the words with long <u>u</u> and silent
<u>e</u> in a group. Write the words on the
chart.

2. Write the other words on the chart.

Words with Long <u>u</u> and Silent <u>e</u>

_____   _____

_____   _____

_____   _____

_____   _____

_____   _____

Other Words

_____   _____

_____   _____

Spelling Practice Book
© Harcourt • Grade 1 • Book 5

Name _____

▶ **Unscramble the letters to write a Spelling Word.**

1. eus _____

_____

2. uler _____

- - - - - - - - - - - - -

_____

3. ecni _____

4. utec _____

- - - - - - - - - - - - -

_____

5. uebt _____

- - - - - - - - - - - - -

_____

6. bceu _____

- - - - - - - - - - - - -

_____

7. gelar _____

- - - - - - - - - - - - -

8. eutn _____

- - - - - - - - - - - - -

_____

Spelling Words

use
cute
cube
tube
tune
rule
nice
large
hear
talk

▶ **Write the letter or letters that complete each Spelling Word. Then trace the rest of the word.**

9. __ h __ r _____

10. __ t __ k _____

▶ **Read the Spelling Words. Then write each word in the group where it belongs.**

Words with i

_____   _____

-------------------------------   -------------------------------

_____   _____

-------------------------------   -------------------------------

_____

_____

Words with y

_____   _____

-------------------------------   -------------------------------

_____

Words without i or y

_____   _____

-------------------------------   -------------------------------

_____   _____

_____

Spelling Words

my
try
tried
ties
light
might
use
rule
hair
color

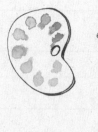

Spelling Practice Book
© Harcourt • Grade 1 • Book 5

▶ **Make cards for the Spelling Words.**
Lay the cards down and read them.

1. Put the words with the long i sound in one group. Write the words on the chart.

2. Write the other words on the chart.

Spelling Words

my
try
tried
ties
light
might
use
rule
hair
color

Words with Long i

_____ _____
- -
_____ _____
- -
_____ _____
- -
_____ _____

Other Words

_____ _____
- -
_____ _____
- -
_____ _____

Spelling Practice Book
© Harcourt • Grade 1 • Book 5

Name _____

▶ **Write the letter or letters that complete each Spelling Word. Then trace the rest of the word.**

1. ___ r ie

2. ___ t ___ s

3. ___ rie

4. ___ ha r

5. ___ c i r

6. ___ se

▶ **Write two Spelling Words that rhyme with kite.**

7. _____

8. _____

▶ **Write two Spelling Words that rhyme with pie.**

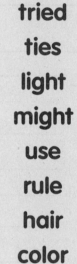

9. _____

10. _____

Name _____

▶ **Read the Spelling Words. Then write each word in the group where it belongs.**

Spelling Words

how
cow
down
out
found
round
try
light
earth
table

Words with <u>ow</u>

_____   _____

_____   _____

_____

Words with <u>ou</u>

_____   _____

_____   _____

_____

Words without <u>ow</u> or <u>ou</u>

_____   _____

_____   _____

_____   _____

▶ **Make cards for the Spelling Words.**
Lay the cards down and read them.

1. Put the words with <u>ow</u> in one group.
   Put the words with <u>ou</u> in another
   group. Write the words on the chart.
2. Write the other words on the chart.

Spelling Words

how
cow
down
out
found
round
try
light
earth
table

Words with <u>ow</u>	Words with <u>ou</u>
_____	_____
------------------	------------------
_____	_____
_____	_____
------------------	------------------
_____	_____
_____	_____
------------------	------------------
_____	_____

Other Words

_____	_____
------------------	------------------
_____	_____
_____	_____
------------------	------------------

Spelling Practice Book
© Harcourt • Grade 1 • Book 5

Name _____

▶ **Write the letter or letters that complete each Spelling Word. Then trace the rest of the word.**

1. 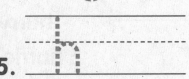 _ou_

2. 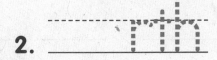 _rth_

3. _igh_

4.  _c w_

5. _h_

6. 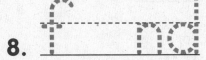 _ta le_

7. _tr_

8.  _f nd_

Spelling Words

how
cow
down
out
found
round
try
light
earth
table

▶ **Unscramble the letters to make a Spelling Word.**

9. dnrou _____

_____

10. owdn _____

_____

91

▶ **Read the Spelling Words. Then write each word in the group where it belongs.**

Words with <u>y</u>

_____   _____

_____   _____

_____   _____

_____

Words without <u>y</u>

_____   _____

_____   _____

_____

Spelling Practice Book
© Harcourt • Grade 1 • Book 5

Name _____

▶ **Make cards for the Spelling Words. Lay the cards down and read them.**

1. Put the words with the long <u>e</u> sound in one group. Write the words on the chart.

2. Write the other words on the chart.

Spelling Words

funny
happy
story
stories
hurry
hurried
how
out
baby
done

Words with Long <u>e</u>

_____   _____
------------------   ------------------
_____   _____
------------------   ------------------
_____   _____
------------------   ------------------
_____   _____
------------------   ------------------
_____

Other Words

_____   _____
------------------   ------------------
_____   _____

Name _____

▶ **Write the letter or letters that complete each Spelling Word. Then trace the rest of the word.**

1. _____ t

2. d _ ne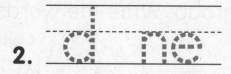

3. hap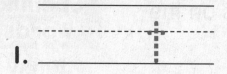

4. st ry

5. ow

6. stor s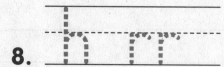

7. b b

8. h rr

Spelling Words

funny
happy
story
stories
hurry
hurried
how
out
baby
done

▶ **Unscramble the letters to make a Spelling Word.**

9. uidrhre
_____
- - - - - - - - - - - - - - - - -
_____

10. yunfn
_____
- - - - - - - - - - - - - - - - -
_____

Ha-Ha-Ha-Ha

Spelling Practice Book
© Harcourt • Grade 1 • Book 5

Name _____

▶ **Read the Spelling Words. Then write each word in the group where it belongs.**

Words with <u>oo</u>

_____ _____

_____ _____

_____ _____

_____

Words without <u>oo</u>

_____ _____

_____ _____

_____

Spelling Practice Book
© Harcourt • Grade 1 • Book 5

▶ **Make cards for the Spelling Words. Lay the cards down and read them.**

1. Put words with the long <u>u</u> sound in one group. Write the words on the chart.

2. Write the other words on the chart.

Words with Long <u>u</u>

_____ _____

_____ _____

_____ _____

_____ _____

_____ _____

Other Words

_____ _____

_____ _____

_____ _____

Spelling Practice Book
© Harcourt • Grade 1 • Book 5

Name _____

▶ **Write the letter or letters that complete each Spelling Word. Then trace the rest of the word.**

1.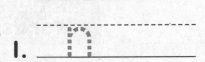

2.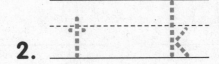

3.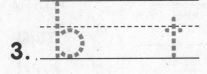

4.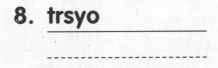

5.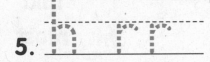

6.

Spelling Words

boot
tooth
soon
noon
new
grew
story
hurry
great
took

▶ **Unscramble the letters to make a Spelling Word.**

7. ttoho _____

8. trsyo _____

▶ **Write two Spelling Words that rhyme with <u>moon</u>.**

9. _____

10. _____

97

Name _____

▶ **Read the Spelling Words. Then write each word in the group where it belongs.**

Words with i

_____   _____

_____   _____

_____   _____

_____   _____

Words with o

_____   _____

_____   _____

_____   _____

_____   _____

Words without i or o

_____

_____

Spelling Practice Book
© Harcourt • Grade 1 • Book 5

▶ **Make cards for the Spelling Words. Lay the cards down and read them.**

1. Put the words with long <u>i</u> in a group.
Put the words with long <u>o</u> in a group.
Put the words with long <u>u</u> in a group.
Write the words on the chart.

2. Write the other words on the chart.

Spelling Words

find
mind
mild
cold
fold
most
soon
new
boy
building

Words with Long i	Words with Long o

Words with Long u	Other Words

99

Name _____

▶ **Write the letter or letters that complete each Spelling Word. Then trace the rest of the word.**

1. m i d

2. c l d

3. b o

4. f n d

5. m n

6. f o

7. e w

8. b l d i n g

Spelling Words

find
mind
mild
cold
fold
most
soon
new
boy
building

▶ **Unscramble the letters to make a Spelling Word.**

9. stmo
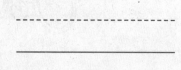
_____

10. noso
_____

100

Spelling Practice Book
© Harcourt • Grade 1 • Book 5

Name _____

▶ **Read each sentence. Look at how the two words are spelled. Fill in the circle next to the correct word.**

SAMPLE: Mom made up a _____ story.

    ○ funnie   ● funny

1. A cat was very _____.

    ○ colde   ○ cold

2. Robert _____ out to play.

    ○ hurried   ○ hurryed

3. He and Bonnie _____ the cat.

    ○ fownd   ○ found

4. It _____ to lick Robert's hand.

    ○ trighd   ○ tried

5. They picked up the _____ cat.

    ○ cute   ○ coot

▶ **Read each pair of sentences. Look at how the underlined words are spelled. Then fill in the circle next to the correct sentence.**

SAMPLE: ● We eat at <u>noon</u>.
○ We eat at <u>newn</u>.

1. ○ I'll be <u>happy</u> when we eat.
   ○ I'll be <u>hapy</u> when we eat.

2. ○ Let's <u>finde</u> a snack.
   ○ Let's <u>find</u> a snack.

3. ○ My big <u>tooth</u> is loose.
   ○ My big <u>towth</u> is loose.

4. ○ Is it hard to bite <u>doun</u>?
   ○ Is it hard to bite <u>down</u>?

5. ○ It <u>miht</u> fall out.
   ○ It <u>might</u> fall out.

Spelling Strategies
Look for word families.

These words are a family.
- Words in a word family rhyme.
- The first letters are different.
- The other letters are the same.

Word families can help you spell words.
- Think about the beginning sound of the word you want to spell.
- Write the letter that stands for this sound.
- Think of a word in the same word family.
- Write the letters that are the same.

I want to spell

The letter <u>h</u> stands for the beginning sound.

<u>Pen</u> is a word in the same word family.

I'll add the letters <u>en</u> and write <u>hen</u>.

Spelling Practice Book
© Harcourt • Grade 1

Word Sort Cards

Write a Spelling Word in each box.

Cut out the word cards. Sort the words.

See how many ways you can sort the words.

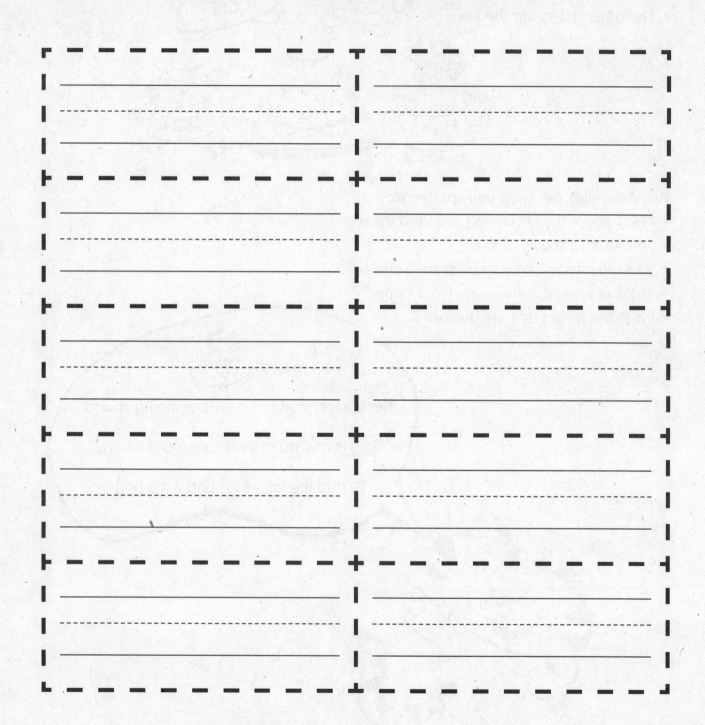

Spelling Practice Book
© Harcourt • Grade 1

Handwriting

Manuscript Alphabet

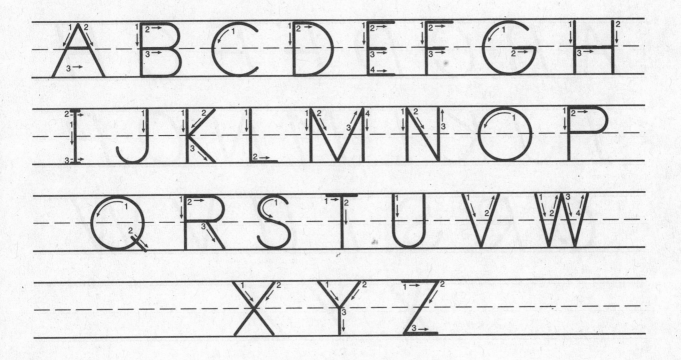

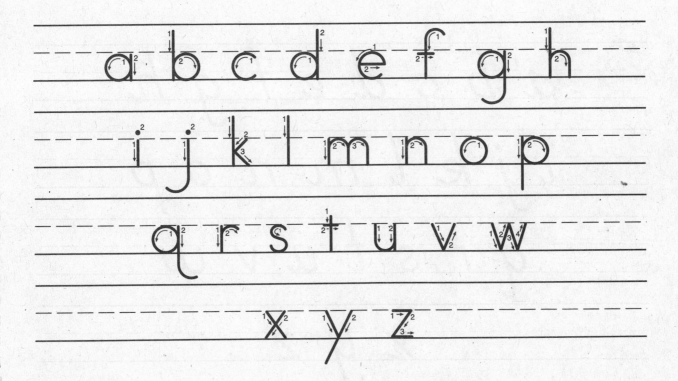

Handwriting

D'Nealian Manuscript Alphabet

A B C D E F G H
I J K L M N O P
Q R S T U V W
X Y Z

a b c d e f g h
i j k l m n o p
q r s t u v w
x y z

Spelling Practice Book
© Harcourt • Grade 1